All global publishing rights are held by

Ukiyoto Publishing

Published in 2025

Content Copyright © Ukiyoto

ISBN 9789370097483

All rights reserved.
No part of this publication may be reproduced, transmitted, or stored in a retrieval system, in any form by any means, electronic, mechanical, photocopying, recording or otherwise, without the prior permission of the publisher.

The moral rights of the author have been asserted.

This is a work of fiction. Names, characters, businesses, places, events, locales, and incidents are either the products of the author's imagination or used in a fictitious manner. Any resemblance to actual persons, living or dead, or actual events is purely coincidental.

This book is sold subject to the condition that it shall not by way of trade or otherwise, be lent, resold, hired out or otherwise circulated, without the publisher's prior consent, in any form of binding or cover other than that in which it is published.

www.ukiyoto.com

FOREWORD

The book, Kauravendra Duryodhan explores the many shades of Duryodhan—prince, warrior, friend, and antagonist—through evocative short stories and poetry. Often cast solely as a villain, he is reimagined here with nuance and depth, inviting readers to see beyond the lines of dharma and adharma. These narratives give voice to his ambitions, loyalties, and inner conflicts, challenging us to reflect on power, pride, and perspective.

This is not a defense, but a rediscovery. May each page provoke thought, stir emotion, and offer a fresh lens on one of the Mahabharata's most complex characters.

Valmiki Goswami,
Professor & HOD,
History Department
University of Guwahati

contents

Duryodhana, the Villain of Mahabharata *By Devajit Bhuyan*	1
The Rise and Fall of Suryaveer Thakur *By Aurobindo Ghosh*	7
I am Duryodhana! *By Mahendra Arya*	17
Duryodhan: The Unyielding Prince *By Manmohan Sadana*	20
Jealousy! Thy name is Duryodhan... *By Kajari Guha*	36
Duryodhan Rebooted *By Purnima Dixit*	41
Why Not Me and Other Poems *By Rhodesia*	52
The Tiger Prince in Chains: A Lament of Hindustan *By Dr. Renuka KP*	58
Venerating the Vanquished Villain *By Dr. Alokparna Das*	65
A Second Chance *By Aryan Majumder*	69
Duryodhan - The Deprived *By Sujata Chaudhuri*	77
About the Authors	80

Duryodhana, the villain of Mahabharata

By Devajit Bhuyan

King Subala of Gandhar (now Afghanistan) was reluctant to give marriage of his daughter Gandhari to blind king Dhritarashtra. He was right but due to persuasion by Bhishma and fearing the might of Kuru Kingdom, finally Subala agreed for the marriage. With the mistake of his father, Gandhari made the blunder by deciding to remain blindfolded throughout life as her husband couldn't see the world. Gandhari was not born blind but became blind by default for the decision of her father.

When a child was born to a blind royal couple without any parental monitoring and control, the consequences are well known. Being born blind, Dhritarashtra was resentful, jealous, arrogant and revengeful. And with his DNA it was quite natural that his son Duryodhana was born with similar qualities. Neither mother nor father could see the bad and inappropriate way how their son grew and adopted all the bad qualities of royal family, and the blind parents made their eldest son a pampered boy. The wrong decision of Subala to agree marriage of his daughter to blind king Dhritarashtra and blunder of Gandhari to remain in forced blindness created a character Duryodhana and later he became the most hated villain of Mahabharata.

Duryodhana was jealous in nature, greedy for power and highly egoist. Though he took education under the same guru Drunacharya along with five Pandavas, he was jealous to Bhima and Arjuna since the days of gurukul as in skill of warfare he was always behind them. The myth is that when Pandavas built their capital in Indraprastha, seeing the beauty of the palaces and the capital, Duryodhana became too much jealous to Pandavas and decided to grab the kingdom of Pandavas by hook or by crook. His maternal uncle Shakuni, who was also considered as another villain of Mahabharata war along with Duryodhana and Dhritarashtra took the opportunity of the jealousy and greed of Duryodhana to settle old score and take advantage of the situation with his clever, crooked mind and deceiving tricks.

Along with the bad qualities of his father Dhritarashtra, Duryodhana also inherited some of the good qualities of his mother Gandhari. He was loyal to his friends like Karna whom he made a king to grow as a competitor of Arjuna and to Pandavas family. In Mahabharata, Duryodhana was portrait as a man of jealousy, ambition, arrogance, ruthlessness, and instigator of conflict. All his good qualities were overshadowed by his bad qualities. He never listened to the advice of his seniors and teachers like Bhishma, Druna, Bidur and other learned ministers of his kingdom, rather he fully depended on the advice of his maternal uncle without realizing the basic intension of his uncle. It is always easy to instigate, manipulate arrogant and ambitious people with apple polish and Duryodhana showed total immaturity and became a puppet in the hands of Shakuni. One of the basic characteristics of Mahabharat was that the decisions of the king was binding on all advisers, ministers and noblemen of the kingdom and in front of arrogant and greedy Duryodhana, the big figures like Bhishma and Durna remained helpless when Duryodhana ordered removing clothes of Draupadi in the king's parliament in presence of everybody. This incident put Duryodhana in bad light among all his subjects and people started to consider him a villain rather than a brave king and protector of woman.

The arrogance of Duryodhana and his hatred to Pandavas was so high that, the king who donated a part of his kingdom to Karna, refused to concede five villages to Pandavas. Neither his father nor mother nor Bhishma could persuade Duryodhana to give away five villages and avoid the war. In this matter also he had prevailed by his trusted adviser Shakuni above all noblemen of the kingdom. Gandhari the blind mother by default neither tried to stop the war deliberately or ignored it or failed to persuade Duryodhana. The environment of upbringing, genetic DNA from Dhritarashtra and manipulation by own maternal uncle created the biggest and most hatred villain of the Epic Mahabharata.

Though Duryodhana was considered to be the main villain of Mahabharata and the person behind the destruction of Kuru clan and their kingdom, in reality, it was his father Dhritarashtra who was equally responsible for Kurukshetra war. Like his blind eyes, Dhritarashtra always put blind eyes to the misdeeds of his son Duryodhana. In the incident of fraudulent dice playing, burning of the Laksha Griha (house of lac) to kill Pandavas, removing clothes of Draupadi and other deceitful activities of his elder son, Dhritarashtra always silently supported his son out of love and affection. Due to the mistakes of father and mother and circumstances of the time, Duryodhana became a victim of situation and convert to a hatred villain of Mahabharata. The author of Mahabharata tried to absolve Dhritarashtra being blind and old at the time of war from portraying him as an equal villain like his son Duryodhana, but reality is that both are two sides of the same coin.

It is said that Dhritarashtra had strength of thousand elephants and his jealousy to his own cousin was so much that he tried to crash the head of Bhima knowing that Bhima was superior to Duryodhana in warfare of ***Goda.*** After losing the war of Kurukshetra, Duryodhana was hiding in a lake and to bring out him from the hiding place, Bhima abused him to hurt his ego and then Duryodhana came out of his hiding to fight with Bhima. This proved that egoist Duryodhana was not coward in nature but ready to face challenges hands on when his ego is hurt. Duryodhana could never tolerate rejection by any one and he eloped with Bhanumati, when she rejected him in the ***Svayamvara.*** Subsequently Bhanumati agreed to merry Duryodhana after reaching Hastinapura. Duryodhana justified his act giving example of his great grandfather Bhishma who abducted three princes of Kashi.

The story of Mahabharata is still considered to be the story for establishing justice, truth and rule of Dharma. However, the story line of the epic is full of deceit and falsehood to achieve the goal of justice and truth. Duryodhana alone was not responsible for the war but due to his vocal character and being the king of Hastinapur, he had to accept the fall out of defeat in the Kurukshetra war. Losing leaders are always orphan as no one want to take share off defeat and discredit. Duryodhana was also not exception. Overall, the character of Duryodhana was very complex in Mahabharata and he remained as a symbol of jealousy, ego, arrogance, greed and ambition making him the number one villain in the story of Mahabharata. There are lots of things to learn from the character of Duryodhana for avoiding ego, jealousy and arrogance for a better life.

In Bhagavad Gita Sri Krishna explained to Arjuna about five factors involved in all actions by a human being- the body, the I-sense of the performer, senses, expression of energy through them and the fifth, the unknown, incalculable uncertainty. This uncertainty is beyond control of any human being. This uncertainty is explained by Physicist Heisenberg in modern quantum physics as "Heisenberg's Uncertainty Principle" which is one of the pillars of modern physics. Sri Krishna also explained about three types of nature of human beings that control and motivate his actions. They are Sattva, Raja Tama. The Rajas knowledge dominated by direct attention to the diversity of things and not their unity, work dominated by it results in actions done with great attachment, egoism and expenditure of energy; an agent dominated by it is greedy, cruel, attached and subject to elation and depression;

intelligence dominated by it is riddle with confusion about right and wrong and has little sense of duty; strength dominated by it is under the sway of ambitions, desires and worldly status. Anti-social work is done by persons with demoniac nature (Asuri-Sampat). Everything they do is for ostentation and self-aggrandizement and no form of cruel exploitation and selfish indulgences is repugnant to them, provided their pleasure, profit, ambition are promoted thereby, and ego is satisfied. Duryodhana was a perfect Raja type of human being with demonic nature and destined to doom.

The Rise and Fall of Suryaveer Thakur

(A Tale of Power, Arrogance, and Betrayal)

By Aurobindo Ghosh

Suryaveer Thakur, the younger son of Himanchal Pradesh's Chief Minister Chandraveer Thakur, was born into privilege. He was raised in opulence, accustomed to people obeying his every command. From an early age, he understood that power was inherited, not earned. His father, Chandraveer Thakur, was a veteran politician who ruled the state with an iron grip. While his elder brother, Dharamveer, was quiet and reserved, Suryaveer thrived in the limelight, enjoying the perks of being a leader's son. His father and the Chief Minister Chandraveer Thakur knew that taking advantage of his position, his son Suryaveer was engaged in some underground dealings with some mafia dons to grab some quick money. Many a times Chandraveer tried to dissuade his son from those unethical activities, but Suryaveer did not heed to his father.

Their family name commanded respect, but Suryaveer was well aware that it was respect built on fear. Their father's loyalists, bureaucrats, police officers, and even businessmen knew better than to cross the Thakur brothers. With an army of loyal henchmen and limitless money, they were untouchable especially Suryaveer. To punish anybody for petty reasons was day to day action of this younger son of Chandraveer Thakur. Chandraveer was more dependent on his younger son than Dharamveer because in politics, fear in the minds of general people gives an edge in democratic system of governance.

Suryaveer Thakur was not just another politician's son; he was born into power and privilege. His father, the Chief Minister of Himanchal Pradesh, ensured that his every wish was fulfilled, and by the time he was in early twenties, he was treated like royalty. Servants, teachers, and even law enforcement officers bowed before him, reinforcing his belief that he was superior to everyone around him. He grew up in an environment where people did not question him but obeyed him out of fear. Over time, this sense of entitlement got transformed into an unshakable superiority complex.

Superiority Complex and Opportunism

Suryaveer did not see people as individuals with their own identities and aspirations; he saw them as tools to be used or obstacles to be crushed. Every situation, whether in politics, business, or personal relationships, was an opportunity for him to manipulate others for his benefit. He surrounded himself with people who constantly flattered him and never questioned his actions. These sycophants fueled his ego and ensured that he remained blind to his own faults.

Within the political party, he maintained control through a careful mix of fear and rewards. Those who remained loyal to him were rewarded with positions of power, government contracts, and protection from law enforcement. However, if someone dared to defy him or even suggest an alternative approach, he ensured their political ruin. On one occasion, a senior party worker, who had been loyal to his father for decades, suggested that Suryaveer should present a more approachable image to the public. Instead of taking the advice in stride, Suryaveer reacted with open contempt. In the middle of a party meeting, he threw a glass of water on the man's face and accused him of trying to weaken his authority. Without a second thought, he ensured that the man was stripped of all his responsibilities and humiliated within the party ranks.

Suryaveer's sense of superiority was not limited to his political dealings but extended to his personal relationships as well. His so-called friends were not people he trusted but individuals who depended on him for political favors. Anyone who showed signs of independence or popularity became a threat. When a young MLA from his party, Aditya Rawat, started gaining a strong following among the youth, Suryaveer saw him as a challenge rather than an asset. Instead of fostering an alliance, he spread rumors that Aditya was involved in an illicit affair with a foreign female journalist. He even planted a British woman to testify. After blaming Aditya, she left for London with hefty sum of money never to return to India. Within days, the scandal ruined Aditya's career, forcing him to resign. When Aditya pleaded for help, Suryaveer smirked and reminded him that power belonged to those who knew how to hold it, not those who relied on goodwill.

Disrespect for Women and Elders

Despite his charm and political influence, Suryaveer had no respect for women. He did not see them as equals but as trophies to be possessed or as political assets to be used when necessary. Whenever a female colleague presented a political strategy, he dismissed her opinions with a smirk, making it clear that he believed politics was a game of power that women were not suited for. He frequently made promises to women activists and leaders within the party, but when the time came to deliver, he either ignored them or ensured that they remained dependent on him for further opportunities. The ladies were given posts in the Panchayat Samiti or at Zilla Parishad level and not beyond that.

One of the most glaring examples of his disdain for women in politics was his treatment of Ananya Sharma, a young and dynamic leader who was gaining popularity in the youth wing of the party. During a crucial meeting, Ananya challenged one of Suryaveer's policy decisions, arguing that the party needed to connect with grassroots workers rather than rely solely on elite politics. Suryaveer saw her as a direct threat to his authority and orchestrated her downfall. Overnight, a fake scandal was manufactured against her, and negative stories flooded the media. By the time Ananya realized what was happening, she had lost her credibility. When she confronted Suryaveer and accused him of ruining her career, he merely smiled and told her that she was better suited for magazine covers than for Vidhan Sabha. She left politics for good. The nation lost a firebrand woman potential leader.

Suryaveer's arrogance extended to his own family, particularly his elder brother, Dharamveer. Unlike Suryaveer, Dharamveer was a man of principles, well-read and ethical. While their father admired intelligence of Dharamveer, Suryaveer saw his brother as weak and incapable of handling real power. Whenever Dharamveer tried to offer a fair and just perspective, Suryaveer mocked him. He often told him that kindness and integrity had no place in politics. When Dharamveer expressed concerns about their father's declining health and suggested that they should focus on his well-being rather than on political games, Suryaveer dismissed him without hesitation. He coldly remarked that their father's funeral would be a grand political event, implying that even death could be used as a tool for their advantage. Suryaveer listened to only one person, his maternal uncle Keshav Deb Singh. Keshav Dev was an expert drug dealer based in an unknown place. Only very knew his activities including Suryaveer. Mamaji was very clever. All the transaction and deliveries were executed in the name of Suryaveer because no law enforcement personnel would block the movement of Suryaveer's consignments.

His relationship with his sister-in-law, Vaishali, was equally strained. Vaishali was sharp, ambitious, and politically astute, qualities that Suryaveer found threatening. He could not manipulate her the way he controlled others, which led him to despise her. When she expressed a desire to enter active politics, he made it clear that she was only successful because she had married the right man. He refused to acknowledge her intelligence and frequently undermined her contributions. At a public event, when Vaishali was giving a speech about women's empowerment, Suryaveer interrupted her with loud laughter and leaned over to a journalist, making a snide remark that she should focus on empowering her husband before talking about politics. His statement went viral, but instead of apologizing, he insisted that it was just a joke.

Power, Politics, and Greed

Vaishali was the daughter of a senior leader in their father's party. Unlike Dharamveer, Vaishali was ambitious, sharp, and ruthless. She saw politics as her domain and quickly became the unofficial strategist for both brothers. Her influence over the family strengthened when her father – in-law and her own father began encouraging her to enter active politics against the will of Suryaveer.

Initially, though Suryaveer, already an arrogant warmonger, found a perfect political ally in Vaishali and both saw politics as a game of dominance, where manipulation, aggression, and elimination of rivals were the keys to victory; but soon he found a competitor in Vaishali in political battlefield. But he kept low for the benefit of the family's political stronghold.

Under their father's guidance, both Suryaveer and Vaishali contested the state elections. Their campaigns were fueled by money, muscle, and their family's legacy. Suryaveer's aggressive, no-nonsense approach attracted young, disillusioned voters, while Vaishali's calculated outreach made her a force among women and the educated class. When the results were declared, both won their seats and became MLAs.

The Battle for Power

When the time came for cabinet formation, the party high command made it clear; only one of them could be given a ministerial berth. The dilemma shook the Thakur household. Both Suryaveer and Vaishali were power-hungry and unwilling to step aside. Their respective fathers, who once encouraged their rise, now found themselves caught between political storms within the family.

The battle lines were drawn.

- Suryaveer believed he was the natural choice because of his lineage, aggression, and ability to maintain dominance.
- Vaishali, however, argued that she had a wider appeal and a sharper political mind. She had earned her place, not inherited it.

Dharamveer, caught between his wife and his brother, remained silent. He had no interest in power, but he saw the brewing storm. Vaishali did not like the attitude of her husband. She expected his vocal support which she missed.

The War Begins

Suryaveer, blinded by ego and a superiority complex, began sabotaging Vaishali's image within the party. He used his father's old loyalists to spread rumors that Vaishali was too ambitious and untrustworthy. He openly disrespected her, mocking her rise as a "borrowed power" from her father and husband.

Vaishali, however, was no less ruthless. She played the long game, secretly gathering allies, even within Suryaveer's camp. She approached their father's political rivals, hinting at a possible shift in loyalties. Her strategic moves forced the party high command to reconsider their decision.

The media caught wind of the family rift, turning it into a political spectacle. Opposition leaders mocked the ruling party for failing to control its own people. Publicly, Chandraveer Thakur tried to maintain a neutral stance, but behind closed doors, he struggled to choose between his son and his daughter-in-law. In between, news came that Vaishali's father is not neutral. He was in consultation with party high command.

The Betrayal

When the final decision was made, it was a brutal blow to Suryaveer; Vaishali was given the ministerial berth. The party saw her as a better long-term investment. Suryaveer was furious. His father tried to pacify him, offering him a bigger role in the next election, but he felt betrayed. He couldn't accept that a woman, his brother's wife, had outplayed him.

Enraged, he lashed out. He began openly criticizing the government, attacking Vaishali in private meetings, and even hinting at forming his own faction. His frustration turned into recklessness. He started using his muscle power to instill fear again, but the tides had already turned. The same people who once feared him now saw him as a liability.

The Downfall

Vaishali struck the final blow when she silently and secretly exposed Suryaveer and his Mamaji's illegal dealings; land grabs, contract rigging and hidden offshore accounts. The opposition parties pounced on the evidence, and the media turned against him. His father, realizing the damage, distanced himself. Dharamveer, who had remained silent throughout, finally spoke choosing his wife over his brother. Suryaveer was left with no allies, no power, and no way out. His empire collapsed. His name, once feared, became a joke.

The Endgame

Suryaveer's fall took multiple paths. He was expelled from the party for two years. With mounting cases against him, he was arrested and released on bail, His legacy reduced to court hearings and legal battles. Unable to accept defeat, he lost himself in vices alcohol, drugs, and self-imposed exile until he faded into obscurity.

Suryaveer's story is a testament to how unchecked ego and entitlement can lead to self-destruction. He was given everything; power, wealth, fear but he lost the one thing he always craved: respect. In the end, he was not defeated by his enemies, but by his own arrogance and inability to adapt. As he stood alone, watching his empire crumble, he finally understood the bitter truth. The very people he had crushed were now the ones writing his political obituary. His belief in his own superiority had been his greatest strength, but in the end, it was also his ultimate downfall.

Epilogue

In the history of mankind, there was another similar character. His name was Duryodhana. He too had the similar traits as Suryaveer Thakur. Duryodhana too had the same fate. He too was lost without any trace.

i am duryodhana!

By Mahendra Arya

A hated person ! A wicked ruler!
An unleashed wild animal getting crueler!

What made me that, I sometimes wonder!
Am I responsible for all that blunder!

Not really, I get my answer!
There were others who made me the chancer!

A Father- blind by birth who could not see me ever
But blind by mind too, who forbade me never!

A mother – who was needlessly blind
Copying my father she too lost her mind!

And the army of my ninety-nine brothers
Who gave me a superiority complex over others!

An uncle Shakuni, who acted like a reptile
Who taught me his wickedness and poisonous smile!

And my great friend Karna, who too was a loser
Just a friend, but neither the guide nor a philosopher!

And the Pandavas! I hate them for being spineless!
In the name of Dharma, they became useless!

And that addict gambler Yudhistir! Walked into my trap!
Knowing fully well, my chessboard and the cunning map!

And the elders in my court, were just the eye witness
As they lacked in their character the much-needed moral fitness!

Dronacharya! My Guru! Who lived on my maintenance!
So much obligated, could not utter even a sentence!

Bhishma! My unmarried grandfather!
Just registered his protests but could not go any farther!

Draupadi! She did not even exist for me, until
She ridiculed me with a sharp tongue and shrill
She got some sadistic pleasure in abusing me and my father
Without realizing my wrath will go much farther!

Duhshashan! My stupid brother! Went a little too far!
In obeying my order to humiliate Draupadi in my Darbar!

Krishna! He was always biased towards Pandavas
Was a wrong choice for mediation with me, Alas!

Vidur! The only sensible and virtuous person around me
Being just a singular, could never ground me !

I am not responsible for what I became
There are lot many people, I just mentioned each name !
I too was born in this world, like any other child
Became a devil who was uncivilized and wild!

Duryodhan: The Unyielding Prince

By Manmohan Sadana

In Hastinapur's gilded halls of pride,
A prince was born with eyes defiant wide.
Duryodhan, heir of Kuru's throne,
His heart a stone, yet not alone.
The son of blind king Dhritarashtra's line,
Raised with a fire that sought to shine.

Beside him, Pandu's children grew—
Five brothers righteous, brave, and true.
Arjuna's aim, Bhima's might,
Yudhishthir's vow of truth and right.
Nakula, Sahadeva, shadows bright,

Perfect sons in Dharma's light.

But what of he, the darkened star,
The one who bore fate's cruel scar?
Was Duryodhan the villain cast,
Or a mirror of the world, too vast?

The Game of Dice, the Game of Life

Yudhishthir gambled Dharma's name,
Duryodhan laughed, but who took shame?
Was it the prince who sought their fall,
Or Dharma's son who staked it all?

Who truly sinned, who bore the stain—
The gambler or the one profane?
For Duryodhan, the crown his right,
He saw Pandavas not as light,
But rivals born of different womb,
Seeking to plunge him to his doom.

In court he stood, his head held high,
While Draupadi's shame filled the sky.
A moment dark, forever known,
Yet how many such moments we own?
In boardrooms, courts, or narrow lanes,
The Draupadis still voice their pains.

Duryodhan's laughter echoes loud,
But so does that of every crowd

That sees a woman stripped of pride,
And turns away, or stands aside.

Bhima's Wrath, Arjuna's Skill, Yudhishthir's Moral Will

Each Pandava bore a gift divine,
Bhima, the strength of every line.
His hunger vast, his rage untamed,
Yet for his wrath, none ever blamed.

Arjuna's arrows split the skies,
Praised for valour, never lies.
Yet it was he who rained down death,
While Duryodhan fought for every breath.

Yudhishthir, Dharma's righteous face,
Yet he gambled away his grace.
Sahadeva, Nakula, noble, kind—
But even they left no peace behind.

And Duryodhan? The flawed, the vile?
Or simply human all the while?
A brother fierce, a friend so true,
To Karna, none such friendship knew.

Karna's Bond: Loyalty and Loss

Karna, son of Surya's light,
Raised in darkness, shunned by right.
Duryodhan saw not caste or birth,
He crowned his friend, gave him worth.

In that, his noblest deed was cast,
A bond of brotherhood meant to last.
For in a world of masks and guile,
Duryodhan wore his hate with style.

He did not feign, he did not hide,
His loves, his hates, were all his pride.
What he could not win, he sought to claim,
For he knew no other way to fame.

The Battlefield: Kurukshetra's Cry

And so they met where dharma bled,
The field where fathers, brothers, wed
Their fates to war, to blood and fire,
Each driven by a different pyre.

The Pandavas fought with Krishna's hand,
The god who shaped both sea and land.
Duryodhan stood with might and men,
But gods don't walk with mortal kin.

In water's womb he made his stand,
His body shielded by Gandhari's hand.
Yet fate, relentless, found its path,
Bhima's mace unleashed his wrath.

And down he fell, the prince of pride,
With Karna gone, with all denied.
Yet dying, still he did not weep,
No coward's death, no soul asleep.

Duryodhan Today: The Modern Shade

What then remains of Duryodhan's name?
Is he but a shadow cast in shame?
Or does his tale, once steeped in rage,
Still haunt the dreams of this new age?

In boardrooms cold, in parliaments vast,
In leaders born of ancient caste,
In every man who fights his fate,
And every heart consumed by hate.
He lives in those who won't let go,
Who see the world as friend or foe.
In those who battle born divides,
In every son whom fairness hides.

Yet Duryodhan, for all his sins,
Reminds us all where rage begins.
In being told, you are less than,
Denied the right to dream, to plan.

His flaw was pride, his curse was birth,
But not his dreams, nor his worth.
He sought the crown, he sought the sky,
And fought until it was time to die.

Who Then is Righteous, Who the Knave?

The Mahabharata does not save
A single soul from judgment's eye,
The gods themselves must justify.
For each a hero, each a fiend,
And dharma's lines are never clean.

So Duryodhan, the world's dark face,
Still walks with us, still seeks his place.
In every protest, every cry,
In every dream we let to die.

He is the one who speaks aloud,
Who dares to stand against the crowd.
Not always right, but never small,
His rise, his rage, remembered all.

The Tale Concludes, But Lessons Stay

And so we see in Duryodhan's fall,
Not just a prince, but one of all.
The Pandavas, heroes bright and grand,
Yet flawed as he, by human hand.

In him we see our own descent,
Our dreams betrayed; our anger spent.
Our modern wars, our broken dreams,
Our chasing after hollow schemes.

Yet also strength, the will to fight,
To claim the dark, not just the light.
For history is not merely won
By those who walk where bright skies run.

It's shaped by those who dared defy,
Who chose to live, who chose to die.
And in that fight, Duryodhan stands—
Not just a foe, but s shrewd man.

The Battle of Threads

The city of Amritsar was buzzing with the success of YouthWear, a clothing brand run by the Randhawa cousins. Bright colors, trendy designs, and affordable prices made their brand the talk of Punjab's young crowd. But behind the smiling faces of the Randhawas, there was one man waiting—Preet Singh.

Preet was their cousin, tall, proud, with a sharp mind and an even sharper tongue. He believed YouthWear was his birthright. After all, hadn't his father once run the family business before losing everything to a bad investment?

One afternoon, Preet stormed into the YouthWear office, his face red with anger.

"Where's Vijay?" he barked.

Vijay Randhawa, the eldest of the cousins, came out of his cabin. "What now, Preet?"

"You think you all can build this empire while I watch from the side? My father started all this! And you pushed us out!"

"Preet, enough! We built YouthWear from scratch. The old business died long ago. You weren't even interested back then."

Preet smirked. "I was busy studying the market, Vijay. I know more about the youth fashion industry than your whole team."

"So, what do you want?"

"A partnership. Forty percent share."

Vijay laughed. "Forty? Are you out of your mind?"

Preet's eyes narrowed. "You'll regret this insult, Karan."

And thus began Preet's war.

Within weeks, Preet launched YouthStyle, a rival brand. Same designs, same price, but with one difference—he copied every successful YouthWear design and released it a week earlier.

"How's he doing this?" Simran, Vijay's sister, asked in frustration. "Every new design we finalize, he releases it before us."

Vijay rubbed his temples. "He has a mole in our team. Someone's leaking information."

Meanwhile, Preet was enjoying his success. Sitting in his newly furnished office, he grinned as he saw his sales climbing.

"Good Job, boys," he told his team. "Keep pushing. I want YouthWear out of the market."

His manager hesitated. "Sir, we're burning cash on these campaigns. If this continues…"

"I don't care," Preet snapped. "My cousins need to learn their place."

The Randhawas were losing customers. Orders dropped, and social media was full of comparisons.

"Vijay," Simran said one evening, "maybe we should talk to him. Offer him something?"

"No," Vijay said firmly. "He's not here for money. He wants to destroy us."

"But what if he does?" she whispered.

"We'll fight."

Preet grew bolder. He bribed YouthWear's delivery team, causing shipments to delay. He spread rumours online about their quality. He even sent fake customers to post bad reviews.

One day, Preet cornered Vijay outside the Golden Temple.

"How's business, brother?" he sneered.

Vijay clenched his jaw. "We're still standing."

"Not for long," Preet grinned. "Give me what I asked. Join me, or I'll finish you."

"You'll fail, Preet. You can copy our designs, but not our spirit."

"We'll see."

But Preet's overconfidence became his weakness. His own team, tired of his arrogance, started making mistakes. Orders were mixed up, customers complained, and soon YouthStyle's image suffered.

Meanwhile, Vijay found the mole—one of the designers, bribed by Preet. Vijay fired him quietly and shifted operations.

"Enough is enough," Vijay declared. "Let's go back to what made us strong. Unique designs, limited editions, quality focus."

Simran nodded. "And I'll handle the social media. No more rumours, no more silence."

Slowly, YouthWear bounced back. Their new campaign, "Be Original, Wear Original", caught the youth's attention.

Preet panicked. "Slash the prices!" he ordered.

"But sir, we're already running losses—"

"Do as I say!"

Finally, the market decided. YouthStyle collapsed under debts, poor reviews, and bad publicity. Preet sat alone in his office, staring at the empty chairs.

His manager entered, looking grim. "Sir, the suppliers want their money. Staff is leaving. It's over."

Preet laughed bitterly. "They all left me. Even my own blood."

The next morning, Preet showed up at YouthWear.

"Here to surrender?" Vijay asked coldly.

Preet smirked. "You won. But I hope you know... I've left cracks in your company. It won't be the same."

Vijay stared at him. "You fought like Duryodhan, Preet. Brave, but blinded by ego. You couldn't win because you never believed in building—only destroying."

Preet shrugged. "Maybe. But I'll rise again."

"Do whatever you want," Vijay said quietly. "We'll survive."

Preet walked away, defeated but not broken.

Months passed. YouthWear grew stronger, but they often found hidden issues—angry suppliers, confused customers, small glitches. Preet's shadow remained.

One evening, Simran asked Vijay, "Do you think he'll ever stop?"

Vijay sighed. "No. People like him don't stop. But neither will we. But we should remember the famous couplet by Bashir Badr:

Shourat ki bulandi bhi pal bhar ka tamasha hai

Jis daal pe baithae hoe, who toot bhi sakti hai

(Zenith of fame is a momentary spectacle,

The bough on which you are sitting can break also.)

Thus, in the heart of Amritsar, the battle of threads continued—between pride and perseverance.

jealousy! thy name is duryodhan...

By Kajari Guha

The quote "Frailty, thy name is woman!" borrowed from Shakespeare's renowned tragedy, "Hamlet", has ever been a good source of portraying a female character for those who believe in male chauvinism. If we change the words a little, like "Jealousy, thy name is Duryodhan!" It would be sufficient to feature all the negative aspects of Duryodhan's nature. However, what were the causes that had been instrumental in shaping his character like this are well known to most who have gone through the epic, the Mahabharata. This feeling, called jealousy, is, more or less, inherent in all the human beings. Duryodhan is also not an exception to this, but what led him to make life so difficult is the question that has to be answered.

The Mahabharata, the great epic, depicts the war between two groups, the Kauravas and the Pandavas. They belonged to the royal background and were cousins. The eldest of the Pandavas was Yudhisthira who had four brothers named Bhim, Arjun, Nakul and Sahdev. He was a staunch supporter of Dharma.

He never deviated from the path of honesty, but as a sharp contrast Duryodhan, the eldest brother of Kauravas with his ninety nine siblings has been portrayed as a trickster and the catalyst who brought an end to the Hastinapur dynasty that belonged to the Kauravas.

When Duryodhan was born, it is said that many untoward incidents happened that were ominous, but his blind father Dhritarashtra doted on him and called him Suyodhan affectionately. However his name Duryodhan suggests "someone who is extremely difficult to wage war against", hence Duryodhan sharing all the responsibilities of his ninety nine siblings and the mother Gandhari who used a blindfold to show her immense love and respect to her blind husband. In a nutshell, Duryodhan had all the qualities of a good soul, but sibling rivalry and the influence of his wicked maternal uncle Shakuni changed his mindset that posed him as a villain.

Jealousy signifies resentment. It refers to bitterness and hostility towards a person, a group, a community or a nation because they have some special qualities, characteristics or attributes or some materialistic possessions that you don't have. Jealousy is synonymous with envy, but envy defines mostly negative feelings mixed with admiration and discontent. In a nutshell, jealousy implies a deeper anguish than envy. It generates a sense of uneasiness and distress and involves coveting what someone else possesses or owns. It is like a "green-eyed monster" giving vent to unhealthy emotions.

The conflict arose from the very beginning as Dhritarashtra was blind and the eldest of the three brothers, i.e. Dhritarashtra, Pandu and Vidura. Dhritarashtra could not be the king of Kuru dynasty as he was blind and Pandu became the ruler and earned a lot of name and fame as a ruler.

Dhritarashtra was married to Gandhari, and Pandu was married to Kunti and Madri. Kunti gave birth to Yudhishthira, Bhim and Arjuna. Madri became the mother of Nakul and Sahadev. Gandhari's pregnancy continued for a long time. She became very angry and upset. She thought that Kunti's son would now be the heir to the throne. She started beating her womb and gave birth to a lump of flesh.

Sage Vyasa cut the flesh into hundred pieces and kept each of them in a pot immersed in ghee.

Then he buried them underground and after a year they emerged as hundred sons. Duryodhan was the eldest among them. Yudhishthira was elder than him and was crowned as the king of Kuru dynasty after his father's death. All this caused a lot of confusion in the mind of Duryodhan. Moreover, Shakuni, his maternal uncle, instigated him against his cousins. It was all because of power and wealth. The mundane materialism caused havoc in his life. Another factor was very much responsible to transform his behavior towards the Pandavas, who were his own cousins and were not driven by ego and all negative influences.

Envy and rivalry

Pandavas were strong. They were popular. They were virtuous. Bhima and Arjuna were more skillful in warfare than Duryodhan. Their strength and popularity made him feel insecure and gave birth to envy and rivalry.

Legacy to Hastinapur's Throne

Duryodhan expected that he would be crowned to the throne of Hastinapur, as he was the eldest son of Dhritarashtra, but Yudhishthira was the eldest son of Pandu. Thus he was believed to be the legitimate successor. This enraged Duryodhan a lot.

Jibes in Indraprastha

Once Duryodhan visited Pandava's palace in Indraprastha. The floor was extremely shiny. Duryodhan thought it to be a water pool and lifted his clothes to avoid. However, he got confused about the solid ground and fell into the actual water pool. It is said that Draupadi and others mocked at him and said, "The son of a blind man is also blind." This aggravated his hatred towards the Pandavas and his ego got hurt.

Shakuni hated Pandavas.

He always told Duryodhan that he had been betrayed by Pandavas. They had snatched the throne from him. This enraged Duryodhan more and more .Shakuni was the one who played the most active role in featuring Duryodhan's negative aspects of character.

Game of Dice

Shakuni organized the heinous dice game and Duryodhan played it with Pandava. In this game, Yudhishthira lost his kingdom, fortune and even his wife, Draupadi. Duryodhan lost control of his manners and arrogantly insulted Draupadi. This resulted into the eternal enmity between him and the Pandavas.

Exile and Return

Pandavas lost the dice game. Duryodhan exiled them for thirteen years and thought they would never come back to Hastinapur again. They came back and wished to get the share of the kingdom for which they were eligible. However, Duryodhan refused to do so and this led to the great Kurukshetra war.

Finally, Duryodhan's arrogance, jealousy, greed and ego were the consequence of his surroundings and the people who brought them up. They say, "A man is known by his company." And Shakuni had always been with him from his childhood supporting him with a source of negative energy, hence justifying the statement, "Jealousy! Thy name is Duryodhan!"

duryodhan rebooted

By Purnima Dixit

The notification pinged on his diamond-encrusted phone – another thousand followers on Instagram. He smirked, adjusting the silk scarf that draped just so over his impeccably tailored linen shirt. "Another addition of thousand sheep for the shepherd," he murmured, his voice a low rumble that somehow sounded both arrogant and alluring.

Duryodhan "The Unconquerable", as his online persona proclaimed, was a phenomenon. In a world saturated with influencers peddling everything from detox teas to fast fashion, he stood out. His brand wasn't about fleeting trends; it was about unapologetic luxury, unwavering confidence, and a certain regal bearing that seemed to emanate from his very pores.

His sprawling penthouse in Mumbai, was his kingdom, overlooking the Arabian Sea, was the backdrop for most of his content. Floor-to-ceiling windows showcasing the glittering cityscape, opulent furnishings and a walk-in closet the size of a small apartment, overflowing with designer wear that whispered of old money even though it was all his hard earned money not a legacy. Born to middle-class professors parents in Delhi, he'd defied their quiet surprise when he declared his dream of becoming a game developer. They hadn't stopped him from following his dreams.

By day, he coded his magnum opus: a metaverse called Hastinapur. By night, his hobby—daily "Duryodhan's Decree" posts—catapulted him to fame within months he became prominent influencer. One day, it would be a review of a limited-edition Swiss timepiece, his wrist adorned with enough carats to make a jeweler blush. The next, it would be a tour of a private jet, en route to some exotic locale. He'd offer pronouncements on everything from the art of the perfect Negroni to the importance of a bespoke suit, always delivered with an air of absolute authority.

His followers lapped it up. They were drawn to his unapologetic embrace of the finer things, the sense that he lived in a world they could only dream of. *#Duryodhanaesthetic*, *#King*, and *#UnconquerableLife* trended constantly. Brands clamored for collaborations, offering him astronomical sums for a single mention. But beneath the polished veneer and the carefully curated online presence, a familiar restlessness churned within him. He had conquered the digital world, amassed a virtual kingdom of followers, and yet... it felt hollow.

'Hastinapur' remained unfinished, a distant dream. Sometimes, staring into the mirror, he caught a flicker in his eyes—an ancient fury, a shadow of tales his grandmother once spun. Kingdoms denied. Resentments that burned. They felt like myths, yet they haunted his dreams, leaving him sweat-soaked and unsettled.

Another ping: his cousin Yudhishthir's story. The Pandavas had entered GameManiac, a competition to craft virtual worlds where avatars roamed free, owning digital assets and living wild fantasies.

Duryodhan scoffed, he always thought his cousins were far away from this gaming world. **Yudhishthir** was just a low-key mindfulness coach with a surprisingly large following, preached peace and simple living & his brother **Bhima**, a popular fitness coach known for his intense workouts and equally intense honesty, often posted about the dangers of superficiality. **Arjuna**, a travel photographer with an eye for capturing raw beauty, seemed to wander the globe, untouched by the digital frenzy. **Nakul** and **Sahadev**, twin entrepreneurs with a focus on sustainable fashion and ethical technology, maintained a quiet but influential presence.

Duryodhan smirked at their earnestness. "Amateurs," he'd muttered as he regularly used to scroll through their feeds. Now, they dared challenge his domain. Fired up, he poured himself into Hastinapur. His avatar emerged: a towering figure, sharp-jawed, radiating power. A digital realm where he'd reign supreme

"Playing at being virtuous while I build an empire." Now, he was more pumped about being part of the competition. This will help him in building his digital dominion.

But as the metaverse project neared its launch, cracks began to appear in Duryodhan's carefully constructed world. A series of anonymous posts started circulating, questioning the ethics of his endorsements, highlighting the environmental impact of his lavish lifestyle. The comments section of his posts, once a chorus of adoration, began to fill with critical voices. Followers started to unfollow. Brands grew hesitant. The "Unconquerable" image was beginning to fray.

One evening, staring at his avatar in the nearly completed virtual Hastinapura, Duryodhan felt a pang of something he hadn't felt in a long time – vulnerability. This digital kingdom, for all its grandeur, felt even more ephemeral than his online fame.

During presentation of first phase, when different gamers presented their avatars, Duryodhan saw Yudhishthir's avatar, a calm and serene figure meditating in a virtual forest, Bhima's avatar leading a virtual fitness class, his booming laughter echoing through the digital space. He even saw Arjuna's avatar, sketching a breath-taking virtual sunset.

A strange curiosity, a feeling he couldn't quite name, drew him towards Yudhishthir's virtual sanctuary. He hesitated for a moment, his digital hand hovering over the "enter" button. It felt like stepping into a world he had deliberately avoided.

He clicked.

Yudhishthir's avatar opened its eyes and offered a gentle smile.

"Duryodhan," he said, his voice calm and welcoming even in the digital realm. "Welcome."

Duryodhan's sharp wit seemed to desert him. He stood there, his powerful avatar feeling strangely out of place in the tranquil virtual forest.

"What... what is this?" he finally managed, his voice a low growl.

"A space for reflection," Yudhishthir replied simply. "A place to find peace amidst the noise."

Bhima's avatar lumbered over; a virtual sweat towel draped around his neck. "Feeling Lost, Bro?" he asked, a hint of his old teasing in his voice, but without malice.

Arjuna's avatar approached, holding out a virtual flower that shimmered with impossible colors. "Sometimes, the most beautiful landscapes are found when you stop chasing the horizon," he said softly.

Duryodhan felt a wave of unfamiliar emotions wash over him – confusion, a flicker of longing, and something akin to... envy? They seemed content, these cousins of his, even in this artificial world. They had built something real; something that resonated beyond likes and followers.

Envy flickered away—then longing. They seemed... content. Their creations resonated beyond metrics. His own Hastinapur felt like a gilded shell. In that quiet forest, surrounded by their warmth, a seed of doubt sprouted. Peace, he realized, wasn't power—it was simpler, deeper.

Echoes of the Past

He looked at his own avatar, the embodiment of power and luxury, and for the first time, it felt strangely empty. The virtual Hastinapura, his digital dream, suddenly seemed like a gilded cage. The users joined his game didn't look happy.

He didn't know what the future held. His online empire was teetering. His carefully constructed image was cracking. But standing there, in the quiet of Yudhishthir's virtual forest, surrounded by the unexpected warmth of his cousins, a tiny seed of something new began to sprout within Duryodhan "The Unconquerable".

That's moment he realized "peace" is not in gaining more power, but it is actually in simple joys of life.

***

Duryodhan with renewed feelings, redeveloped his "Hastinapur". The lines of code shimmered on his multiple monitors, each a tiny brick in the virtual city taking shape. He meticulously sculpted the digital architecture, the grand avenues and imposing palaces echoing the descriptions from his grandmother's tales – tales he'd always dismissed as fanciful. Yet, as he designed the virtual kingdom, a jolt, sharp and unexpected, would sometimes pierce his focus. A fleeting image of a magnificent hall, impossibly ornate, and a wave of bitter envy so potent it made his stomach clench. He'd shake his head, attributing it to stress, too many late nights fueled by caffeine and ambition. But the flashes persisted. While coding the virtual dice game feature for his metaverse, a chilling vision of loaded dice and Draupadi's horrified face would momentarily overlay his screen. He'd recoil, a cold sweat breaking out on his brow. These weren't mere memories; they were visceral echoes, feelings he couldn't explain, tied to events he intellectually knew but emotionally couldn't grasp.

The development of the digital Hastinapura became a strange form of penance. Every grand structure he created was tinged with a subconscious awareness of its historical counterpart and the darkness that had unfolded within its walls. He found himself subtly altering aspects, adding virtual gardens where the Kauravas court once plotted, designing serene waterways where battle cries once echoed. It was as if his subconscious was attempting to rewrite history within the digital realm.

His interactions with his cousins in the metaverse became increasingly nuanced. He'd still carry a hint of his old swagger, but it was now tempered with a hesitant respect. When Yudhishthir's avatar offered guidance on a particularly complex ethical dilemma within the game's framework, Duryodhan found himself listening intently, the dismissive retort that would have once sprung to his lips remaining unspoken.

He even Initiated a virtual "Pandava Conclave" within Hastinapura, a dedicated space for them to collaborate on projects and share ideas. He'd find himself genuinely interested in Nakul and Sahadev's sustainable fashion initiatives for avatars and Arjuna's breathtaking virtual landscapes. Bhima's directness still occasionally grated, but Duryodhan found himself appreciating his cousin's unwavering honesty, a stark contrast to the sycophancy he'd often cultivated in his real life.

During developing the digital world he would get flashes of past, which were becoming more frequent, more potent. They were forcing him to confront something within himself, a buried sense of guilt and regret that his conscious mind had always fiercely suppressed. He started researching ancient texts online, driven by a compulsion he couldn't explain. He devoured translations of the Mahabharata, his own name and the events surrounding it leaping off the digital pages with a disturbing familiarity.

He began to understand. These weren't just stories; they were echoes of a past life, a past where he had been the architect of his own downfall and the suffering of others. The weight of that past, however fragmented, was beginning to settle upon his modern soul.

As he sat with his cousins bonding over cup of coffee…he couldn't help but wonder, seems "the past has a way of making itself known, even across lifetimes."

Duryodhan looked at his cousins, a sense of connection forming that transcended the digital divide and the weight of their shared, yet unacknowledged, history. He had built this digital kingdom, perhaps subconsciously, as a space for reconciliation, a place where the mistakes of the past could be acknowledged, if not entirely erased.

***

Duryodhan leaned back in his ergonomic chair, a genuine smile playing on his lips as he watched Bhima's avatar attempt a complicated virtual yoga pose in the Pandava Conclave, his digital limbs flailing hilariously.

"Careful there, Bhima," Duryodhan typed, adding a laughing emoji. "Wouldn't want you to break the metaverse."

Bhima's avatar straightened abruptly, a playful scowl on his face. "Says the guy whose virtual palace probably has more polygons than the entire Amazon rainforest. At least I'm trying to find some inner peace, unlike someone who's probably plotting world domination, digital or otherwise."

Arjuna's avatar chuckled, sending a string of applause emojis. "He's got a point, Duryodhan. Remember that time you tried to install a 'KauravaCoin' as the sole currency in Hastinapura?"

Duryodhan rolled his eyes, a fond exasperation in his gesture. "That was a strategic initiative to boost user engagement! Besides, Yudhishthir vetoed it faster than you can say 'dharma'."

Yudhishthir's calm avatar interjected, a gentle smile in his digital eyes. "Prudence prevailed, Duryodhan. Though I must admit, the initial concept was... ambitious."

Duryodhan found himself laughing along with them, a genuine, unburdened sound. This was new. In his fragmented memories, interactions with his cousins were fraught with tension, veiled insults, and simmering resentment. This easy camaraderie felt... liberating.

***

Later that week, Duryodhan video-called Karna, his best friend and his partner, his closest confidante, a web developer with a knack for turning Duryodhan's extravagant visions into digital reality.

"So, the 'Pandava Conclave' is actually working?" Karna asked, a hint of surprise in his voice as lines of code scrolled across his screen. "Last I heard, you were virtually building moats around your digital palace to keep them out."

Duryodhan chuckled. "Old habits die hard, my friend. But... things are different now. Those... flashes I told you about? They're becoming clearer. I see... a different version of myself. Not a pleasant one."

Karna paused his coding. "You mean the 'evil cousin' stories your grandma used to tell?"

Duryodhan nodded, a shadow passing over his face. "It feels... real, Karna. The anger, the envy... I can almost taste it. And it's horrifying. I don't want to be that person again. In any life."

"So, the 'Unconquerable' is trying for a redemption arc?" Karna raised a skeptical eyebrow, but there was a hint of genuine curiosity in his eyes.

"Something like that," Duryodhan admitted.

"Yudhishthir... he has a way of making you see things differently. And the others... their genuine goodness... it's... infectious, in a way. I want to use my platform, my influence, for something... better. To be a good example, as you said. The opposite of that... other Duryodhan."

Duryodhan actively sought out opportunities to collaborate with his cousins online and even in the real world. He partnered with Nakul and Sahadev on a campaign promoting sustainable digital practices, using his massive platform to amplify their message. He even agreed to participate in one of Bhima's intense charity fitness streams, much to the amusement of their followers.

Duryodhan found himself relaxing in their company, the weight of his past life – the life he was only beginning to truly understand – feeling a little lighter in their presence.

Why not me and other poems

By Rhodesia

Why Not Me?

At times, another person towers before us,
Imposing attention and commanding respect,
But at the back of our mind, a startling thought stirs,
As seeds of inadequacy blooms in the heart.

When faced with somebody more charming and lovely,
Whose poise and stance exhibit stunning elegance,
At the back of the admiration, we question -
Why is she endowed with dazzling beauty, not me?

When someone else's purse overflows with silver,

And he can afford anything his heart desires,
When his lifestyle elevates and his trade prospers,
Why such luck befalls on another, we wonder.

Perhaps the comparison that brings utmost pang,
Is when somebody else receives the attention,
Admiration, warmth, tenderness, and affection
Of the person to whom our devotion belongs.

When we look at our reflection in the mirror,
And we see staring at us, the green-eyed monster
Of insecurity, envy, and jealousy,
We're consumed with a pervasive thought - *why not me?*

The Pitfalls of Insecurity

Like clouds that block the natural light of our soul,
Comparison dims the essence of our being,
Whereas each is endowed with his own vibration,
A particular hue just one person can bring.

Some create a replica of others in them,
Mimicking someone else's style, fashion, and form,
Albeit losing themselves to keep up with the trend,
When they could have shone with their own contribution.

Whereas other people wallow in resentment,
Striving to negate the victor's development,
Searching for misdeeds in a successful man's past,
Vigilantly watching out for any mishap.

Jealousy, to any fondness, is a poison,
A threatened affection that may throttle and own,
While genuine love seeks to do good to a person
A misplaced trust begets lingering suspicion.

At the peak of anger, violence may ensue,
A culmination of fury long overdue,
A pernicious despair that's allowed to fester,
Boiling over hurtful words, actions, and temper.

A Paradigm Shift

All emotions that spring from a person's bosom,
Joy and despair, love and envy or jealousy,
Carry within them a message of wisdom,
Urging an action, with a burst of energy.

Should we be attentive to the whispers of heart,
Instead of suppressing what we deem negative,
And truly listen to the message they impart,
We can have a novel, refreshing perspective.

When we look upon others with admiration,
We see in them an aspect kindred to our own,
A quality we recognize with approbation,
An affinity, but not a comparison.

When we see in others thriving and abundance,
And we feel a rising flame burning from within,
It's our higher self bidding us for a challenge,
To realize our hidden, long-forgotten dreams.

When we feel a pang for our loved one's attention,
It is a proof to the depth of our devotion,
A dormant energy that's stirred into motion,
To be channeled to sweeter acts of affection.

The Tiger Prince in Chains: A Lament of Hindustan

By Dr.Renuka KP

Within the magnificent palaces of Shahenshah Shah Jahan, where golden motifs adorned the ceilings like celestial maps, four sons thrived with youthful energy, each secretly yearning for the imperial throne that seemed within reach as their father aged.

Foremost among them was Murad Baksh, a prince of imposing stature and inherent pride – the Shadow Prince of Hindustan. He was not the eldest; that honor belonged to Dara Shikoh, a scholarly and thoughtful man often immersed in philosophical studies. Nor was he the most cunning; that trait belonged to Aurangzeb, a strategist with a cold and calculating intellect. Murad possessed a different quality: a passionate spirit barely contained by his silken robes; a warrior inclined towards conquest rather than intrigue. His booming laughter echoed through the marble halls, his displeasure could unsettle even seasoned commanders, and his pride was sharper than any Mughal blade.

Murad firmly believed that the throne was a right to be won through strength, not simply inherited by birth order. "The empire rightfully belongs to the most valiant, not merely the firstborn!" he declared one evening, emboldened by wine, as the shadow of his father's mortality loomed. Deep within, he felt a powerful sense of destiny, as if Fate itself had whispered, "It must be you, Murad. You are the true lion of Hindustan."

In those uncertain times, Murad enjoyed the respect of the soldiers. When he rode through their camps, clad in vibrant green armor with a scarlet sash flowing behind him, the men would offer enthusiastic greetings: "Hail Murad Shah! Hail the Tiger Prince!" Their loyalty was a powerful asset in the unfolding succession drama.

Aurangzeb, ever the discreet architect of intricate plans, observed him with meticulous attention. He recognized that Murad's pronounced pride could be both his greatest strength in a potential power struggle and his ultimate weakness if manipulated.

Then, sensing the opportune moment as Shah Jahan's health wavered, Aurangzeb approached Murad with a seemingly sincere and persuasive offer. He suggested they unite to overcome their eldest brother, Dara Shikoh, and his "insubstantial ambitions" for the throne (meaning Aurangzeb viewed Dara's claim as weak). Aurangzeb proposed a strategic alliance: Murad would govern the prosperous region of Gujarat, providing him with power and resources, while Aurangzeb himself would ascend the imperial throne after their victory. He presented this as them being "equal sovereigns" in their respective domains, working together to secure their futures. His smooth and persuasive tone was deliberately charming and deceptive, preying on Murad's ambition.

Murad, fiercely ambitious and hungry for glory in the anticipated succession, was thrilled by this prospect of immediate power and future influence. He eagerly agreed to Aurangzeb's plan, enthusiastically declaring that together they would achieve great things ("cleave the very heavens!"). This impulsive decision showed how easily Murad fell prey to Aurangzeb's manipulation, driven by his desire for recognition and a significant share of the empire in the coming power shift.

However, while Murad envisioned a fraternal partnership in the aftermath of their father's eventual passing, Aurangzeb merely considered him a temporary tool on his own path to absolute power.

The ensuing civil conflict, sparked by the uncertainty of succession, erupted with the force of a monsoon deluge. Murad and Aurangzeb decisively defeated Dara Shikoh at the Battle of Samugarh. Murad fought with a ferocity that seemed divinely inspired – a whirlwind of flashing steel, his war elephant an unstoppable force crushing enemy ranks, his banners snapping like fiery flames.

In the triumphant encampment, Murad stood resplendent, his chest heaving with the exhilaration of victory and the anticipation of his promised reward. "Now," he declared, his voice ringing with conviction, "now our pledged accord must be honored! The empire shall be partitioned according to our agreement! Gujarat shall be my sovereign domain, and from that powerful base, the world shall acknowledge my authority!" He believed the time for their agreed division had come with their victory in the succession struggle.

Aurangzeb offered a slow, chilling smile. "Indeed, my brother. But first... a libation to our shared destiny." His words held a sinister double meaning, masking his true intentions regarding the future division of power.

Murad drank deeply, oblivious to the insidious poison not within the wine, but within the deceptive camaraderie offered under the shadow of their father's declining health. That night, as he rested in a tent filled with intoxicating dreams of future dominion, Aurangzeb's soldiers surrounded him. The metallic clink of chains encircling Murad's wrists shattered the stillness before the dawn sun illuminated the ravaged battlefield, a stark symbol of the brutal realities of succession. The Shadow Prince had been betrayed in the very moment of his perceived triumph in the struggle for power.

Conducted in heavy iron fetters to the fortress of Gwalior, Murad's enraged cries echoed like those of a captive lion, a lament against the injustice of the succession politics. "Traitor! Usurper! This is not justice! The empire will forevermore curse your name!" His cries reverberated against the unyielding stone walls, yet the world beyond had already begun to forget him in the wake of Aurangzeb's ascendance.

Within the oppressive darkness of his prison cell, Murad's mind became a theater of internal conflict, dwelling on the lost opportunity for power in the ongoing succession. Initially, he was consumed by an unyielding rage, striking his fists against the obdurate stones until his knuckles were raw, a futile expression of his profound fury at being outmaneuvered in the succession game. Subsequently, recollections would intrude – the glorious triumphs, the grand processions, the resounding drums accompanying the adulatory cheers of the populace as his name was extolled as a potential future ruler.

"I was destined for a greater purpose than this," he would murmur into the suffocating void, his dreams of imperial power now a cruel mockery. "I was born to be a king." However, his pride, once an emblem of his strength in the succession race, had metamorphosed into the very shackles that confined him, blinding him to Aurangzeb's treachery.

Occasionally, sleep offered a deceptive respite in the form of dreams. In these nocturnal visions, Murad occupied the resplendent Peacock Throne, the weight of the world seemingly pressing upon the crown that adorned his brow in his imagined future as emperor. Courtiers offered deep bows, armies presented arms, and Hindustan flourished under his equitable rule. At other times, he would dream of that starlit night when he and Aurangzeb had pledged their allegiance in the context of the unfolding succession. He would recall the spectral warmth of Aurangzeb's hand in his, the illusory sensation of brotherhood in their joint ambition. "Was I so naive?" he would question the silent walls, the answer lost to his isolation.

Years elapsed with agonizing slowness; the succession now firmly decided against him. Murad became emaciated, his once robust physique a mere vestige of its former vigor. The generals who had once acclaimed him as a powerful contender now served Aurangzeb, the new emperor. The poets who had once lauded his valor now composed panegyrics for his betrayer, celebrating Aurangzeb's victory in the succession struggle. Yet, Murad's spirit, though severely diminished, never truly succumbed to the despair of his lost ambition.

In his final days, when even the hardened custodians felt a flicker of pity for the fallen prince, a faint smile touched Murad's lips. "Convey to Aurangzeb," he whispered to a timorous young boy who attended to his cell, "convey to him that the throne he occupies is accursed. A throne founded upon treachery in the pursuit of power offers no tranquility."

When Murad ultimately perished, isolated in his forgotten cell, no grand obsequies marked his departure from the world of imperial contenders. No cannons roared in his honor. No minstrels sang ballads of his bravery in the succession conflict. But somewhere, in the untamed territories beyond the reach of empire and crown, the wind carried a hushed lament, a melody only the aged soldiers could still recall:

"He was the true lion, a contender for the throne. He waged battle with his entire being for the right to rule. He fell – yet he never yielded his spirit."

History, as is its wont, was recorded by the victor. Aurangzeb reigned for an extended period, his control over the empire becoming increasingly stringent, yet his dominion ultimately rendered it fragile and hollow, a testament to the instability born from treachery in the succession. The brilliance of the Mughal era waned after his demise, crumbling like ancient marble exposed to an unrelenting sun.

But Murad? Murad became a legend. Among the soldiers who understood true valor in the fight for power, among the common populace who recognized inherent strength in a leader, among those who comprehended that sometimes to be vanquished with honor surpassed the triumph of treachery in the succession, the name Murad Baksh endured.

Murad's story tells us that flawed greatness is still greatness and that the line between hero and villain often lies in our perspective. He reminds us to stand tall, even if we fall, and that sometimes, the ones who lose with honor are remembered more deeply than those who win without it. Though Aurangzeb ruled for decades, Murad lives in legend as a tragic but noble warrior.

Venerating the Vanquished Villain

By Dr. Alokparna Das

The lush green countryside soothed my nerves as the car I was travelling in made its way through a narrow highway on a sweltering afternoon. Ramesh, the driver of this vehicle, had voluntarily become a guide in my exploration of Kerala. Working in a content creation company on the outskirts of Thiruvananthapuram, I usually had my weekends off, and often hired Ramesh's car to explore temples, water bodies and hills that didn't find place in the usual tourist itinerary. On one such weekend in the month of March, Ramesh told me about a shrine dedicated to Duryodhan, the main antagonist of the Sanskrit epic Mahabharat. "This must be the only Duryodhan temple in the country," he said, as we started towards Adoor in Kollam district, around 90 kilometres from the state capital. "Well, there's a Duryodhan temple in Uttarakhand's Osla, located on the Har ki Dhoon route," I replied. "Really?" he said. "The

Duryodhan temple in Malanad organises a grand festival around this time of the year. I don't know the exact dates, but if you are lucky, you may get to see the king's chariot. Duryodhan is said to have visited this place and even meditated and prayed at Malanad," he added.

The picturesque route made me wonder what made Duryodhan come to a place that was located more than 3000 kilometres away from his palace in Hastinapur in north India. As we stopped to quench our thirsts at a small hamlet where everyone seemed to be engaged in houseboat-making craft, I asked Ramesh what he feels about worshipping a character like Duryodhan. "I don't know, it is definitely strange. Two years ago, I had taken tourists for an open air Kathakali performance in a temple in north Kerala. The main character of the dance-drama was Duryodhan after he had fallen in the Kurukshetra war," he replied. "Oh, I know that play. It's by ancient Sanskrit playwright Bhash, whose 13 works have been preserved and enacted by the Chakyars of Kerala. That particular play is called Urubhangam or the broken thigh," I told him.

As we entered Malanad, we could hear temple bells and percussion instruments from a distance. The local Kuruva community was all charged up for its annual celebration.

Built in the classical Kerala temple architecture style, the Poruvazhy Peruviruthy shrine had animal figures and colourful umbrellas greeting the visitors. Inside the sanctum, there was no idol but a shining mace placed on a raised and wide platform. Local residents said that Duryodhan came to this place in search of the Pandavas who were in their agyatvas or living in disguise in the final year of their exile. As he searched for the Pandavas in and around this area, Duryodhan was extremely thirsty and asked for water at a small house. An elderly lady offered him toddy, which he is believed to have liked and the drink continues to be offered at this temple. The old woman belonged to a lower caste and realizing that she had offered the drink to a king, she was scared of being punished. However, a grateful Duryodhan seemed unconcerned about her caste and, instead, gifted the local Kuruva community hundreds of acres of land and even prayed for their well-being. The Kuruvas were touched by his gesture and till this date, the shrine built in Duryodhan's honour, pays tax in his name.

The Sun was on his westward journey and it was time for the Malanad Kettukazcha, a celebratory procession of 70 or 80-feet tall and elaborately designed chariot-like structures called Edupu Kala. Percussion instruments started playing as Oorali or the temple priest arrived to bless the displayed items and devotees rushed to carry these structures on their shoulders with the help of long rods. The procession started moving up the hill after encircling the temple thrice. The chariot-like structures were then parked on the hill for the evening performances. With the sun setting on the horizon, Malanad was lit up with thousands of lamps and electric lights. Pity, I thought, there was no way I could stay back for the late night musical performances and other celebrations.

"Next time, we will start early in the morning, so that we can visit the nearby temple dedicated to Shakuni," Ramesh said, as I was about to get inside the car. "What! A Shakuni temple? He is the real villain of the epic. How can there be a temple dedicated to him?" I asked. "Well, the local community believes that after the death of Karna, Shakuni was repentant that he had caused the death of so many soldiers who had nothing to do with the enmity between Kauravas and Pandavas. He came to Malanad and prayed to Lord Shiva so that all the dead soldiers attain moksha or liberation," he said. "But Ramesh, according to the Mahabharat, Shakuni was killed in the Kurukshetra war, how can he come to Malanad to pray for the salvation of soldiers? That's not possible" I protested. Ramesh smiled, "It's difficult to argue when it comes to faith."

The car was crossing Kollam's wetland, the Sasthamcotta Lake. Did Duryodhan visit this place? A man driven by ambition and envy, was he influenced by the pristine natural beauty of the surroundings and thus, underwent a change of heart, playing the role of a benevolent and protective king who valued human kindness? Did the serene splendour of this place turn a villain into a hero to be venerated by generations? My thoughts were interrupted by Ramesh: "So shall we pay a visit to Shakuni in our next trip?" he asked.

"Maybe we can," I smiled.

A Second Chance

By Aryan Majumder

In Kurukshetra's shadowed lore,
Duryodhana, proud, stands tall,
Kaurava prince, with heart of war,
His ambition sparked the fall.Born to Dhritarashtra's line,
Yet blind to wisdom's guiding flame,
He clutched at power, deemed divine,
And staked his soul in envy's game.With Shakuni's dice, he wove deceit,
Pandavas exiled, wronged, and scorned;
Draupadi's shame, his heart's conceit,
A fire of vengeance fiercely born.His friendship held Karna's loyal might,
A bond unyielding, fierce, and true,
Yet pride eclipsed his inner light,

And hatred's path was all he knew.On battlefield, with mace in hand,

He faced the world, unbowed, untamed,

But fate, like Krishna's guiding hand,

Outwove the dreams his will had framed.O Duryodhana, tragic lord,

Your tale's a mirror, stark and grand—

A soul by hubris fiercely scored,

Who shook the roots of Bharat's land.In Mahabharata's timeless verse,

Your name endures, both cursed and famed,

A king, a foe, a human curse,

Forever lost, yet never tamed.

Duryodhan's eyes fluttered open, the sterile scent of antiseptic flooding his senses. He lay in a hospital bed, surrounded by beeping machines and stark white walls that hummed with a strange, mechanical life. Tubes snaked from his arms, and a faint glow from a monitor cast shadows across the room. A gentle voice, soft as a breeze, whispered in his ear, "You've been given a second chance, Duryodhan. Use it wisely." The words lingered, both a promise and a warning, as his vision cleared and he took in the unfamiliar world around him. As his strength returned, Duryodhan learned he was in a sprawling modern city, a place of towering glass structures and ceaseless motion, far removed from the blood-soaked battlefields of his past. The nurses spoke of a miraculous recovery, though they could not explain how he had arrived here, his body unbroken despite the mysteries of his condition. Each day, as he gazed out the hospital window at the city's pulsing lights, memories of his previous life crashed over him like a tidal wave. He saw Kurukshetra's vast plains, stained red with the blood of kin and foe. He recalled his pride, his unrelenting ambition, and the betrayals that had spiraled into the downfall of his empire. The faces of his brothers, his allies, and his enemies—Arjuna, Bhima, Krishna— flashed before him, each a reminder of choices that had led to ruin. The weight of his mistakes crushed his spirit, and in the quiet of the hospital room, Duryodhan wept. Could he ever atone for the sins of his past? Was redemption even possible for one who had orchestrated such devastation?

Determined to seize this second chance, Duryodhan left the hospital and ventured into the city. The streets thrummed with life—cars roared past, their horns a chaotic symphony, while people hurried along sidewalks, their faces buried in glowing devices. The air buzzed with the hum of progress, a stark contrast to the clashing swords and thundering hooves of his former world. He wandered aimlessly at first, overwhelmed by the sensory overload, until he stumbled upon a small art studio tucked between a coffee shop and a bookstore. Inside, the air smelled of paint and possibility. A young artist named Mira worked at an easel, her hands moving with a grace that captivated Duryodhan.

Her paintings were vibrant, alive with colors that seemed to dance on the canvas. When she noticed him lingering, she smiled and invited him to try. Hesitant, Duryodhan took a brush, his hands trembling as he dipped it into crimson paint. The first stroke was clumsy, but as he continued, something within him stirred. He painted scenes from his childhood in Hastinapur—not the warrior he became, but the boy who had once laughed with his brothers, unaware of the rivalries that would tear them apart. Each brushstroke felt like a release, a step toward healing the wounds of his past. Mira became his guide, teaching him to see the world through an artist's eyes. She spoke of beauty in imperfection, of finding meaning in the mundane.

"Art is a mirror," she said one day, her voice soft but firm.

"It shows you who you are, but also who you can become." Duryodhan listened, his heart opening to her wisdom. Through painting, he began to confront his regrets, channeling his pain into creations that spoke of loss, hope, and transformation. As Duryodhan navigated the modern world, he marveled at its relentless pace and technological wonders. Smartphones fascinated him—tiny devices that connected people across continents in an instant. He spent hours in a library, learning to use a computer, his fingers fumbling over the keyboard as he explored the internet. Social media was a revelation, a cacophony of voices sharing stories, dreams, and grievances.

At first, the sheer volume of information overwhelmed him. Posts about wars, protests, and innovations scrolled endlessly, each demanding attention. He saw echoes of his past in the conflicts, but also a new kind of power—one driven not by swords, but by ideas and collective will. The city's diversity challenged his old worldview. In Hastinapur, divisions of caste and clan had defined his reality. Here, people of every background mingled—some with skin darker than his, others with accents he struggled to understand. He met a street vendor from Senegal who shared stories of his homeland, his laughter infectious despite the hardships he described. At a community center, Duryodhan joined a cooking class led by a woman from Mexico, her hands deftly shaping tamales as she spoke of her family's traditions. Each encounter broadened his understanding, forcing him to confront the rigid beliefs he had once held. One afternoon, while walking through a park, Duryodhan overheard an argument between two young brothers. The younger boy, cheeks stuffed with sweets, grinned mischievously as his older brother scolded him.

"You ate my ladoos again!" the elder cried, his face flushed with frustration. The scene struck Duryodhan like a thunderbolt. He saw Bhima in the younger boy's voracious appetite, and himself in the older brother's exasperation. Memories of his own rivalry with Bhima flooded back—their childhood quarrels, the bitterness that had festered into hatred. His heart ached for the brother he had lost to pride and enmity. Approaching the boys, Duryodhan knelt beside them.

"He's your brother," he said to the elder, his voice gentle but firm.

"He may drive you mad, but he's yours to protect, not to fight. Cherish him." The older boy blinked, surprised, then nodded slowly. As Duryodhan walked away, he felt a pang of longing for his own brothers. He wondered if he could have changed their fate, if he had chosen love over power. This encounter lingered in Duryodhan's mind, igniting a desire to make a difference. He began volunteering at the community center, where he met a group of activists dedicated to addressing systemic injustices. They gathered in a cramped meeting room, their voices rising with passion as they discussed poverty, discrimination, and the erosion of human dignity. One activist, a woman named Aisha, spoke of her work advocating for refugees, her eyes blazing with conviction.

"Change doesn't come from silence," she said. "It comes from standing up, again and again, until the world listens." Her words resonated with Duryodhan, stirring a fire he had not felt since his days as a warrior. But this was a different kind of battle—one fought with empathy and persistence, not violence. He enrolled in a local university's evening classes, studying human rights law and sociology. The concepts were foreign at first—terms like "equity" and "intersectionality" felt like a new language—but he devoured the material, driven by a hunger to understand the world's complexities. His professors noted his intensity, unaware of the ancient soul behind his eyes. Ironically, Duryodhan, once a prince who had trampled on the rights of others, became a human rights advocate. He joined Aisha's organization, working tirelessly to amplify the voices of the marginalized.

He attended protests, his deep voice carrying over crowds as he spoke of justice and equality. He wrote articles for local newspapers, his words weaving stories of resilience and hope. In courtrooms, he assisted lawyers defending those who could not afford representation, his presence a quiet force of determination. Through his work, Duryodhan encountered communities that reminded him of the strength he had once admired in his enemies. He met a group of indigenous activists fighting to protect their land from corporate exploitation. Their unity and resolve humbled him, recalling the Pandavas' unyielding spirit. At a women's shelter, he listened to survivors of violence share their stories, their courage inspiring him to advocate for stronger protections. Each experience chipped away at the arrogance of his past, replacing it with a profound respect for humanity's resilience. One evening, Duryodhan attended a community art exhibition organized by Mira. His own paintings hung among others, their bold colors and raw emotion drawing a small crowd. One piece, a depiction of two brothers embracing under a golden sky, caught Aisha's eye.

"This is beautiful," she said, her voice soft.

"It feels... personal." Duryodhan nodded, unable to speak. The painting was a tribute to Bhima and himself, a vision of the reconciliation he could never have in his past life. As the years passed, Duryodhan's life became a tapestry of purpose and connection. He mentored young activists, sharing the lessons of his journey without revealing his ancient origins. He painted, each canvas a step toward forgiveness—of himself, of the world. He built friendships that filled the void left by his lost family, their laughter and debates a balm for his soul. One quiet evening, Duryodhan stood on a rooftop overlooking the city. The skyline glittered, a constellation of human ambition and dreams. Tears welled in his eyes, not of sorrow, but of joy. He had found redemption, not through the dominance he had once craved, but through empathy, creativity, and service. The voice that had greeted him in the hospital echoed in his mind: Use it wisely. He had, and he would continue to do so. In this new world, Duryodhan was no longer the prince of Hastinapur, nor the architect of war. He was a man reborn, his heart open to the possibilities of a life well-lived. With every step, he honored his second chance, knowing that true power lay not in conquering others, but in uplifting them. And as the city pulsed below, Duryodhan vowed to keep fighting—for justice, for connection, for a world where every soul could find their own redemption

Duryodhan - The Deprived

By Sujata Chaudhuri

"Wake up Rishabh!! Get up! You are always late for practise." Mridula admonished. It was a regular habit of her to check on her second son every Sunday morning. The first core that had to be done when the Sun rises at 5.30 am in Vishakhapatnam. Mridula pulled back the curtains on either side of the window. She could see the vast expanse of the ocean where as if a painter had given a stroke of gold with his brush on the canvas. A glimpse of the red Sun can be seen rising just above the water basking with its full strength. Mridula bowed her head, hands clasped towards the mighty Creator.

"Rishabh, get up!" she shouted, "now I'l pour water on your head. Do what you want diligently and sincerely. Do not blame your grandfather for everything."

Rohit, the first scion of the elder son Sushant Gupta and the first grandson of Mr. Devansh Gupta, was enjoying his golf meet. He was casual about his work, restless and trying to figure out a way to bring a crack in his grandfather's business. Mr. Devansh Gupta had given him the post of a Director, but he expected more from his grandfather. He wished to be the CEO of the company, which was deprived from him. Rohit was a good student, meritorious, and wanted to pursue his studies in Mathematics in MIT. He had applied and got a scholarship, but his grandfather (who was the CEO at that time) refused to help him financially. Rohit became bitter, sarcastic, and vindictive.

Rishabh, the second son of Sushant Gupta, was a brilliant sportsman. A tennis player, whose ambition was to play in the Grand Slam. For that he wanted to be coached in a good academy like Rafa Nadal Tennis Academy in Spain or IMG Tennis Academy in Florida, but there also his grandfather refused to help. Finally, he joined Tennis Valley Academy in Vishakhapatnam.

Both the sons, Rohit and Rishabh had a grudge and vowed to take revenge on his grandfather, the great Mr. Devansh Gupta. Their father, Sushant Gupta, was also unhappy, since he was not accepted as the successor of the company due to his sufferance from Guillan-Barre Syndrome which made him crippled and had to take help of a wheelchair. He could feel the anger that was in Duryodhana and shared his grievance.

Mr. Devansh Gupta loved and adored his third grandson, Rupak, scion of his second son Sudhir. He wanted to pass the helm to Sudhir, but he had left the world at a very early age. Rupak was younger than Rohit but elder to Rishabh.

He was also meritorious like Rohit, excelled in school and did further studies in London School of Economics. Devansh Gupta finally passed his baton to Rupak, overriding his other two grandsons. He was made the CEO of the company.

An accident occurred in the Gupta family. Tragedy gloomed in the house. Rupak was hit by another car while driving. The windscreen was smashed but luckily it was not fatal. Shreds of glass hit his head. The two brothers plan was not successful. A streak of Duryodhana's nature can be seen in them. It can be justified. Rohit, despite being the eldest grandson of the elder son, was not given the love, respect, and position that he deserved. He was deprived from studying abroad, becoming the CEO of the company, whereas his younger cousin, Rupak, enjoyed all the privileges. Their grandfather discriminated amongst them.

Duryodhana, the son of Dhritarashtra (who was the eldest and king at that time), was also not loved, given priority in the Kingdom. The neglected, unwanted by all apart from his parents. Did he deserve this? He was the eldest son of the king.

about the authors

DEVAJIT BHUYAN, an electrical engineer and multilingual poet from Assam, has authored over 210 books in 45+ languages. A prolific writer in English and Assamese, his poetry spans diverse themes. He holds multiple literary honors, including "Poet of the Year" awards. Notably, he released 34 poetry books in a single day. Visit www.devajitbhuyan.com for more. *Twitter: @devajit_1861 Instagram: @BHUYANDEVAJIT*

FACEBOOK: Devajit Bhuyan

Aurobindo Ghosh is an M.Sc, M.Phil, Ph.D in Statistics and Ph.D in Economics, Dr. Aurobindo Ghosh is a teacher, trainer and research guide. His first poetry book "Lily on the Northern Sky" bagged the award from Ukiyoto Publishing. He is a regular contributor of Ukiyoto Publisher's anthologies. His solo fictional book, "Bimladadi's Dreams", also published by Ukiyoto Publishing which not only awarded as 'Best fiction book of the year' but also got converted into an audio book. His other solo books, namely, Mystical Honeymoon, Deception Redefined, and Chronicles of Detective Subroto Deb Barman are also published by Ukiyoto Publishing. He also creates acrylic, Warli and Madhubani paintings.

Mahendra Arya, 67 years is an engineer by education. Writing has been his passion in Hindi as well as English. He writes fictions, thrillers, mythology, plays and poetry. His mythological fictions Kaikayi – the Misunderstood Queen and Draupadi Demystified have been extremely popular among his readers. His earlier published books include thrillers like Facebook Friends and Tangents and a Circle . His book The First Scam- Story of Haridas Mundhra was published recently, was about a major scam, which took place after Independence of India. His last published book has been about his research on the famous Indian book Gita, that presents the true original version of Gita with 70 shlokas, whereas present available version contains 700 shlokas.

Manmohan Sadana, a retired Joint Director General (Tourism) Government of India is an author, editor, actor and a mandolinist, whose novel – "Healing Strings" has won various awards which include the "Literary Titan Gold Award", "Golden Book Award", "Ukiyoto Emerging Author Award", "Certificate of Appreciation from Kerala Tourism Mart Society" and "Ukiyoto Book of the Decade Award". He has written many short stories which have been published in different anthologies and books. After superannuation from Government Service, he was a student of Persian for three years in St. Stephen's College, New Delhi and presently he is brushing his theatre skills as a student of renowned Director, Activist and Playwright, Mr. Arvind Gaur, in Triveni Kala Sangam, New Delhi.

Kajari Guha is the winner of International Children's book award. A published author, a poet, a composer and a translator, she is a regular contributor to the anthologies of Ukiyoto Publishing.

Purnima a writer by heart...with thoughts in mind and words on paper, inking emotions through her writings. A writer with passion for simplicity, loves to express her emotions, experiences, and opinions about anything that fascinates her. The world of writing inspires & interests her to paint pictures with words. A literature post-graduate, she has always been an avid reader, which inspired her to start writing. From simply writing reviews of few TV episodes on WordPress, she moved to pen down fictional stories, gradually she developed interest in writing poems, She has been writing since 2015 and desires to follow her passion as Writer. When not writing, you can find her listening to good music, Reading and most importantly watching Korean dramas.

Rhodesia is a Filipina physician, poet, and devoted mother. A former ER doctor and biochemistry professor, she helped establish a medical college and managed COVID-19 response efforts. Once the Philippines' Youngest Author, she recently earned multiple literary and medical awards. She writes to inspire with love, hope, and faith.

Dr.Renuka KP, a retired Tahsildar is a native of Ernakulam district in Kerala state. She is a blogger and has published three books in English and 2two in Malayalam. Her stories have been featured in several anthologies and received many recognitions including Honorary Doctorate and international awards .Her writings have been translated into nine foreign languages.

Dr. Alokparna Das is a journalist, award-winning author, classical musician and teacher. She loves to read, travel and collect antique coins.

Aryan Majumdar is an 18 YO young author already having 3 published books to his name and an aspiring engineer. He is a passionate sportsman playing football and cricket in formal formats. He is an enthusiastic creative content writer as well.

Sujata Chaudhuri was a teacher and is retired at present. She completed her Masters in Anthropology and is passionate about music, specially acoustic instruments.

www.ingramcontent.com/pod-product-compliance
Lightning Source LLC
LaVergne TN
LVHW041537070526
838199LV00046B/1703